I0410002

UIC/WEC JOINT RESEARCH PROJECT ON RAIL DEFECT MANAGEMENT

Analytical Modelling of Rail Defects and Its Applications to Rail Defect Management

David Y. Jeong

U.S. Department of Transportation
Research and Special Programs Administration
Volpe National Transportation Systems Center
Cambridge, Massachusetts 02142

January 2003

EXECUTIVE SUMMARY

This report is the third in a three-part series describing the technical contributions of the Federal Railroad Administration (FRA) and the Volpe National Transportation Systems Center (Volpe Center) to the UIC/WEC (International Union of Railways/World Executive Council) joint research project on Rail Defect Management. The first two reports presented correlations between engineering calculations and rail defect growth test data generated under laboratory and field test conditions. This report discusses some of the applications of these engineering analyses to rail defect management. These applications include: (1) determining rail inspection frequencies based on track condition and usage, (2) estimating limits for rail head wear based on fracture mechanics principles, and (3) applying risk analysis to evaluate different strategies for controlling the risk of rail failures. In the context of this report, risk is the occurrence of broken rails from undetected defects. Although a cost/benefit analysis was not included, the risk examples described in this report provide the foundation for more comprehensive risk analyses which can take into account the consequences and costs associated with broken rails.

The titles of the other reports in this series are:

- Correlations Between Rail Defect Growth Data and Engineering Analyses, Part I: Laboratory Tests.

- Correlations Between Rail Defect Growth Data and Engineering Analyses, Part II: Field Tests.

TABLE OF CONTENTS

1. INTRODUCTION

Broken rails, or rail failures, generally occur from fatigue cracks that form and grow in the rail steel as a result of cyclic forces caused by the repeated passage of trains over the rails. A broken rail may cause a train to derail.

The primary method for controlling the risk of rail failures is rail testing. Rail testing is the continuous search of rail to find defects, in order to allow time for remedial actions to occur ahead of rail failures. Remedial actions may entail protection or repair of discovered defects, removal of defective rails from track, or a temporary restriction on train speed. The search for surface-breaking rail defects can be performed visually, but the search for internal rail defects must be performed with specialized equipment that uses ultrasonic or magnetic induction technology.

The frequencies at which rail tests are conducted tend to vary from one railroad to another, but are usually based on either time (i.e., a certain number of times per year) or traffic tonnage (e.g., every 20 million gross tons). Railroads have evolved their rail testing schedules empirically, based on decades of field experience. Railroads in the United States generally tend to test rail more frequently than is required by the Code of Federal Regulations.

One of the most important factors in determining rail testing frequencies is the rate at which rail defects can be expected to grow. The growth rate of rail defects is relatively slow at first, but increases as the defect becomes larger. As a rail defect enlarges, the chance of detecting it increases, but the load bearing capacity of the rail reduces which increases the risk of rail failure.

Laboratory and field experiments were performed in the United States during the 1980s to examine the growth rate of rail defects. To complement the experimental work, engineering analyses were conducted to model the growth behavior observed in the experiments. One of the main objectives in conducting the experimental and analytical studies is to determine the slow crack-growth life of rail defects. The term "slow crack-growth life" refers to the time or tonnage during which the rate of crack growth under normal conditions is predictable. Moreover, the slow crack-growth life defines the window of opportunity to find a rail defect. Using a validated engineering model, the slow crack-growth life of rail defects can be estimated for varying track, maintenance, and operational conditions.

More recently, field data are being generated to examine the growth rate behavior of defects in modern rails; i.e., rails with head hardening. These experiments are being conducted by the Transportation Technology Center, Inc. (TTCI) at the Facility for Accelerated Service Testing (FAST) under the sponsorship of the Federal Railroad Administration (FRA) and the Association of American Railroads (AAR).

In addition to the FAST data, rail defect growth data for contemporary non-heat treated rail steels are being generated under laboratory conditions through an international research project sponsored by the World Executive Council (WEC) of the Union Internationale des Chemis de fer (UIC, or International Union of Railways). The task of the WEC is to identify projects of common interest that UIC members either have in progress or wish to begin. In 1997, the UIC/WEC began an international research project on Rail Defect Management.[1] In this context, rail defect management refers to the development and implementation of strategies for controlling the risk of rail failures. In 1999, the FRA and the Volpe National Transportation Systems Center (Volpe Center) were invited to participate in this international effort to provide technical support specifically in fracture mechanics analysis of rail defects.

In support of the UIC/WEC joint research project on Rail Defect Management, the Research Designs and Standards Organization (RDSO) of Indian Railways conducted laboratory experiments to study the growth rate of internal rail defects. The experiments were carried out using a test fixture that was designed and built specifically for the UIC/WEC joint research project. Laboratory and field test data for rail defect growth were also generated by Spoornet in South Africa as part of this project.

This report is the third in a three-part series. The previous reports described engineering analyses to model the growth of internal rail defects based on test data generated in the laboratory (Jeong, 2002a) and in the field (Jeong, 2002b). The engineering model was used to calculate rail defect growth rates for detail fractures, tache ovale defects, and squat defects. In general, the correlations between the test data and analyses were reasonable, which provides confidence in the model to calculate realistic rates of defect growth.

This report discusses some applications of the modelling work to rail defect management. Particularly, three applications are described which require knowledge of realistic rail defect growth rates: (1) determining rail inspection frequencies, (2) estimating limits for rail head wear, (3) using risk analysis to evaluate different strategies to control the risk of rail failure.

---

[1] The organizations participating in the UIC/WEC joint research project on Rail Defect Management are: Association of American Railroads – Transportation Technology Center, China Railways – China Academy of Railway Sciences, East Japan Railways, European Rail Research Institute, India Railways – Research Designs and Standards Organization, Queensland Rail (Australia), Railway Technical Research Institute (Japan), Russian Railway Research Institute, Spoornet (South Africa), and US Department of Transportation – Federal Railroad Administration and Volpe National Transportation Systems Center.

2. ENGINERING ANALYSIS OF RAIL DEFECT GROWTH

The behavior of rail defect growth has been studied by collecting laboratory and field data and by developing engineering analysis models. The data are used to establish the general ranges of the defect growth behavior and to provide a check on the realism of the models. The models are used to isolate the effect of various track and operational parameters on rail defect growth behavior.

An engineering model for analyzing the growth of detail fractures was developed by the Volpe Center (Orringer, 1988) during the course of previous research supported by the Federal Railroad Administration. This model was used as the basis to correlate the test data generated in the WEC/UIC joint research project on Rail Defect Management. One of the contributions of the present work is the development of a stress intensity factor for squat defects. The results of these correlations were presented in two separate reports, one describing correlations for laboratory test data (Jeong, 2002a) and the other for field test data (Jeong, 2002b). Moreover, the results of these correlations provide confidence in the model to produce realistic estimates of rail defect growth rate and slow crack-growth life.

Sensitivity studies were performed with the engineering analysis model for detail fracture (DF) growth to examine the effect of various factors on slow crack-growth life and critical DF size (i.e., DF size expected to cause rail failure). In these studies, the slow crack-growth life was arbitrarily defined as the tonnage (in million gross tons, MGT) required to grow a detail fracture from 10%HA to 80%HA.[2] These studies were conducted by setting a baseline value for each factor, and then varying the value from the baseline one factor at a time.

Table 1 lists the various factors and the associated range of values assumed in these studies. The values listed in the table for residual stresses are the magnitudes of the tensile longitudinal residual stress at 10%HA.[3] Rail head wear is considered as a uniform loss of material from either the top of the rail (referred to as vertical head-height loss) or the side of rail (referred to as gage-face side wear). Figure 1 illustrates the results of the sensitivity studies for slow crack-growth life in two ways. First, the length of the bars represents the range of slow crack-growth lives as each factor is varied. Second, the factors are arranged to show the gradation of decreased life from the baseline life. For example, the slow crack-growth life for a temperature differential of 110°F (with all other factors equal to their baseline values) is 8.5 MGT, compared to the baseline of 52.3 MGT. The temperature differential is the difference between the rail temperature and the temperature at which the rail experiences no longitudinal thermal force.

---

[2] In the United States, the sizes of transverse defects, such as detail fractures, are generally given in terms of percent rail head cross-sectional area (%HA) where the percentage is based on the area of a brand new or unworn rail head.

[3] The previous reports in this series (Jeong, 2002a; and Jeong, 2002b) describe how residual stresses are treated in the engineering model.

Table 1. Range of values assumed in sensitivity study for slow crack-growth life of detail fractures.

FACTOR	CRACK GROWTH LIFE		
	Minimum	Baseline	Maximum
TRACK DESIGN AND MAINTENANCE			
Curvature	8° Curve	Tangent	Tangent
Rail section	85 ASCE	136 AREA	155 PS
Track modulus	1 ksi	3 ksi	10 ksi
Vehicle dynamics*	DLF=1.95	DLF=1.85	DLF=1.75
OPERATIONS AND MECHANICAL			
Wheel contact center	Far field side	Gage side	Far gage side
Static axle load	39 tons	16.5 tons	9.9 tons
OTHER			
Temperature difference	$\Delta T =110°F$	$\Delta T =14°F$	$\Delta T =0°F$
Rail head wear	20%HA	0	0
Residual stress	26.25 ksi	8.75 ksi	8.75 ksi
Location of defect	0.05 " below	Nominal	Nominal

* NOTE: DLF refers to the dynamic load factor which is used as a multiplying factor on the baseline value for static axle load.

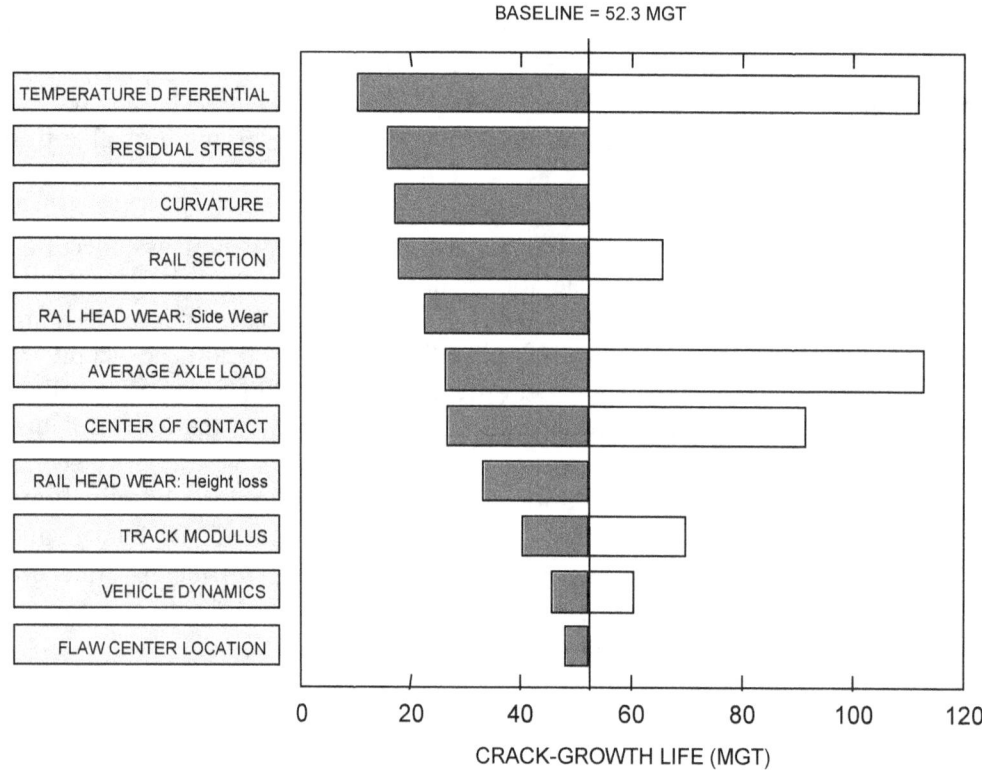

Figure 1. Relative effect of various factors on slow crack-growth life of detail fractures.

Table 2 lists the values assumed in the sensitivity studies to examine the effect these factors have on critical DF size. In these studies, the effect of vehicle dynamics is considered by assuming different multiplying factors on the static wheel load of a locomotive. Moreover, only the reduction of critical DF size from the baseline is considered in the sensitivity studies for critical DF size. Figure 2 shows the results of the sensitivity studies for the critical DF size. For instance, the DF size at rail failure is about 48%HA for the baseline values, compared to 17%HA when the temperature difference is 110°F (with all other parameters equal to the baseline values).

The results from these sensitivity studies indicate that temperature differential and rail residual stress have the strongest effects on slow crack-growth life and on critical detail fracture size. Track curvature has a strong to moderate effect on slow crack-growth life of detail fractures, but a relatively weak effect on its critical size. Axle load, rail section, track modulus, and rail head wear (gage-face side wear and vertical head-height loss) have a moderate influence on detail fracture growth. Vehicle dynamics has a moderate to weak effect on the slow crack-growth life, but a strong effect on detail fracture critical size. The center of wheel/rail contact has a moderate effect on slow crack-growth life, but no effect on the critical size. The location of the flaw center in the rail head has a relatively weak effect on detail fracture growth, and no effect on the critical size.

Table 2. Range of values assumed in sensitivity study for critical detail fracture size.

FACTOR	Critical Detail Fracture Size	
	Minimum	Baseline
TRACK DESIGN AND MAINTENANCE		
Curvature	8° Curve	Tangent
Rail section	85 ASCE	136 AREA
Track modulus	1 ksi	3 ksi
Vehicle dynamics*	DLF=5	DLF=3
OPERATIONS AND MECHANICAL		
Wheel contact center	Far field side	Gage side
Static axle load*	34.75 tons	34.75 tons
OTHER		
Temperature difference	ΔT =110°F	ΔT =14°F
Rail head wear	20%HA	0
Residual stress factor	3	1
Location of defect	0.05 " below	Nominal

* NOTE: Rail failure is assumed to be triggered by an impact load created from a flat locomotive wheel. DLF refers to the dynamic load factor used to magnify the static load.

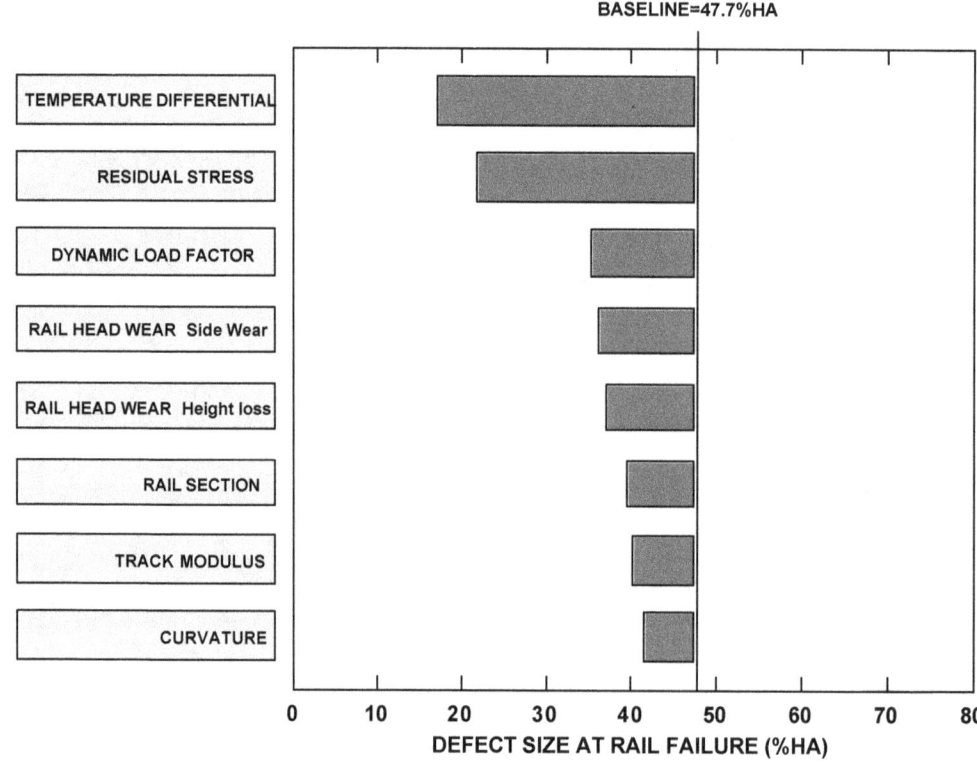

Figure 2. Relative effect of various factors on critical detail fracture size.

3. APPLICATIONS TO RAIL DEFECT MANAGEMENT

Rail Defect Management refers to the development and implementation of strategies to control the risk of rail failures. The primary method to control the risk of rail failures is rail testing through nondestructive evaluation. One of the factors in determining rail test frequencies is the rate at which rail defects are expected to grow.

Rail integrity can be affected by the loss of metal from the rail head or rail wear. A methodology to estimate limits for rail head wear based on fracture-mechanics principles is briefly described in this section.

Risk analysis can be used as a decision-making tool to evaluate the effectiveness of various rail defect management strategies. Two examples of risk analysis which involve the growth of internal rail defects are given in this section.

3.1 RAIL INSPECTION

A guide for scheduling rail tests to detect internal rail defects was developed (Orringer, 1990) on the basis of results produced through research activities sponsored by the Federal Railroad Administration (FRA) in the United States. The guide was designed for self-adaptation to changing track conditions, as reflected by the total rate of detected occurrences per test, the rate of service defect occurrences,[4] and the tonnage of traffic accumulated between tests. In the present context, self-adaptation means that the frequency of rail testing is adjusted on the basis of the observed rate of detected defects and service defects.

The development of the guide was based on the following:

(1)   A performance target of 0.1 service defects per track mile per test is assumed as an acceptable or tolerable level of risk. This number represents the national industry average in the United States over the past fifteen to twenty years.

(2)   A Weibull statistical model is used to estimate the rate at which internal rail defects, such as detail fractures and tache ovale defects, develop in rail. The Weibull distribution has been used to correlate fatigue life data in general since the 1950s (Weibull, 1951) and rail defect data in particular since the 1970s (Besuner et al., 1978).

(3)   The growth rate of internal rail defects is characterized by the slow crack-growth, which is defined as the tonnage to grow a defect from detectable size to a size at which rail failure may be expected to occur under the next train. A value of 40 million gross tons (MGT) is assumed in the guide, and is a factored value based

---

[4] Service defects are defects found by means other than scheduled tests (e.g., commonly when the rail breaks).

on results from engineering analyses validated with experimental data obtained from the Facility for Accelerated Service Testing (FAST) in Pueblo, Colorado, USA. Using a validated engineering model, the slow crack-growth life can be calculated for a specific track condition, maintenance, or operational practice.

(4)   The performance of rail inspection equipment is measured in terms of probability of detecting a defect as a function of its size; the larger the defect, the greater the chance of detection. Figure 3 shows the probability of detection (POD) curve that was assumed in the development of the self-adaptive guide.

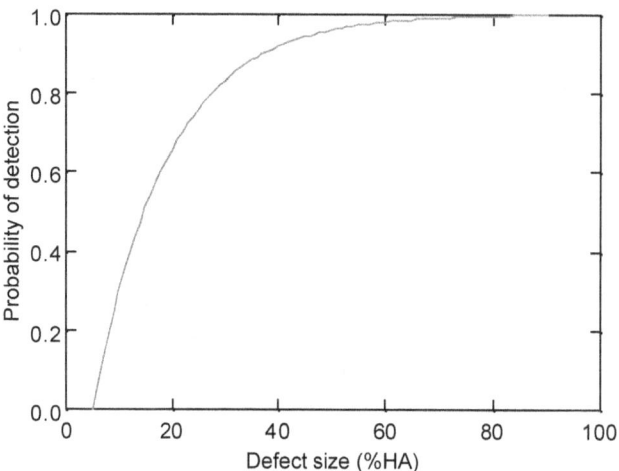

Figure 3. POD curve assumed in the development of the self-adaptive guide for rail testing.

The mathematical relationships composing the self-adaptive guide for scheduling rail tests have been translated into a nomograph, shown in Figure 4. The chart consists of two separate graphs and a central vertical scale. The left-hand graph is used to determine an inspection interval based on the Weibull fatigue life model and the total defect rate. The interval is found by entering the top of the graph at the total defect rate, reading down to the bold blue curve, and then reading across to the central vertical scale. Figure 5 illustrates an example application of the nomograph.

The right-hand graph is used to adjust the inspection interval based on the performance target for acceptable or tolerable service defect rate (i.e., 0.1 service defects per track mile per inspection interval). The adjustment factor is determined by finding the intersection of the vertical line extended from the actual service defect rate and an oblique line extended from the MGT value of the previous inspection interval. The oblique line is drawn parallel to the bold blue guidelines in the graph. Reading across from the intersection to the central vertical scale, the value obtained for the next interval is the inspection interval required to restore the service defect rate to the performance target for acceptable or tolerable level.

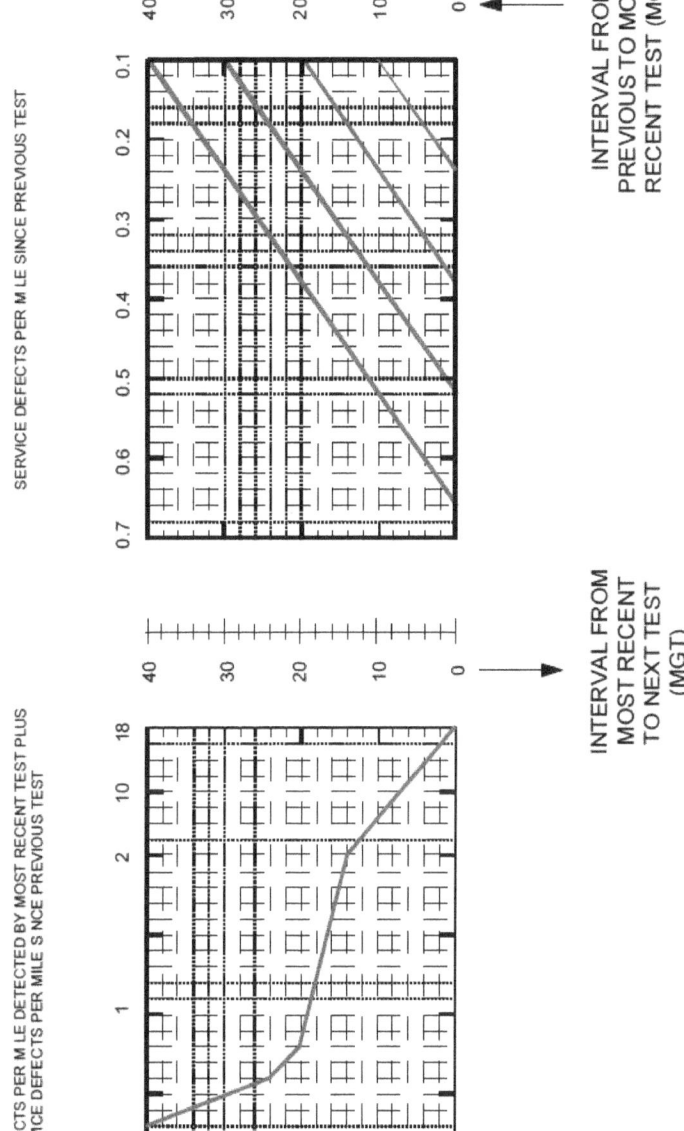

Figure 4. Nomograph for scheduling rail tests.

9

In the example illustrated in Figure 5, rail test intervals are calculated for a hypothetical case in which the service defect rate is 0.14 per track mile in 34 MGT since the previous test, and the most recent inspection detected defects at a rate of 0.40 per track mile. Referring to the left-hand graph in Figure 5, point A is the total defect rate of 0.54 (i.e., 0.14 plus 0.40). Point B is defined by the intersection of a vertical line drawn from point A to the bold blue line in the graph. Reading horizontally across from point B to the vertical scale or point C, the inspection interval based on the total defect rate is 28 MGT. Referring to the right-hand graph in Figure 5, the point D is the service defect rate of 0.14, and point E is the inspection interval since the previous test or 34 MGT. An oblique line parallel to the bold and slanted lines in the graph is drawn to intersect the vertical line drawn from point D, defining point F. Reading horizontally across to the point G, the inspection interval based on the service defect rate is 31 MGT. The average of the inspection intervals based on the total defect rate and the interval based on service defect rate is roughly 30 MGT.

Monte Carlo simulations of rail testing on a hypothetical railroad line were conducted to compare the self-adaptive method as an alternative inspection strategy to testing at constant frequency. The simulations started from newly re-railed track, with the first rail test performed at 100 MGT. Subsequent rail tests were simulated at frequencies specified by the self-adaptive scheduling guide or at constant frequency.[5] A performance target of 0.1 service defects per track mile per rail test and a slow crack-growth life of 40 MGT were assumed in simulating the self-adaptive method for scheduling rail tests.

Two cases were examined: (1) a medium density line carrying 60 MGT per year was simulated for 8 years of hypothetical service, and (2) a heavy haul line carrying 120 MGT per year was simulated for 4 years of hypothetical service.

The results of the simulations are summarized in Figure 6 for the medium density line, and in Figure 7 for the heavy haul line. Both figures consist of four plots as functions of time: (1) the number of rail tests per year, (2) the cumulative total number of rail tests, (3) the detected defects per mile per year, and (4) the service defects per mile per test.

When rail testing is performed at constant frequency on both the medium density and heavy haul lines, the service defect rate per test and the detected defect rate increase exponentially. When the self-adaptive procedure is simulated, the total number of rail tests performed over the duration of the simulation increases (16 versus 21 total rail tests on the medium density line, 16 versus 20 on the heavy haul line). But the benefits of the increased number of rail tests over the long term are: (1) more defects are detected, and (2) the service defect rate is controlled.

---

[5] In its original form (as shown in Figure 4), the guide for self-adaptive scheduling of rail tests (Orringer, 1990) used tonnage between rail tests as an input parameter. The guide can be modified to specify annual tonnage and number of inspections per year rather than tonnage between rail tests. This modification was made to carry out the simulations presented here.

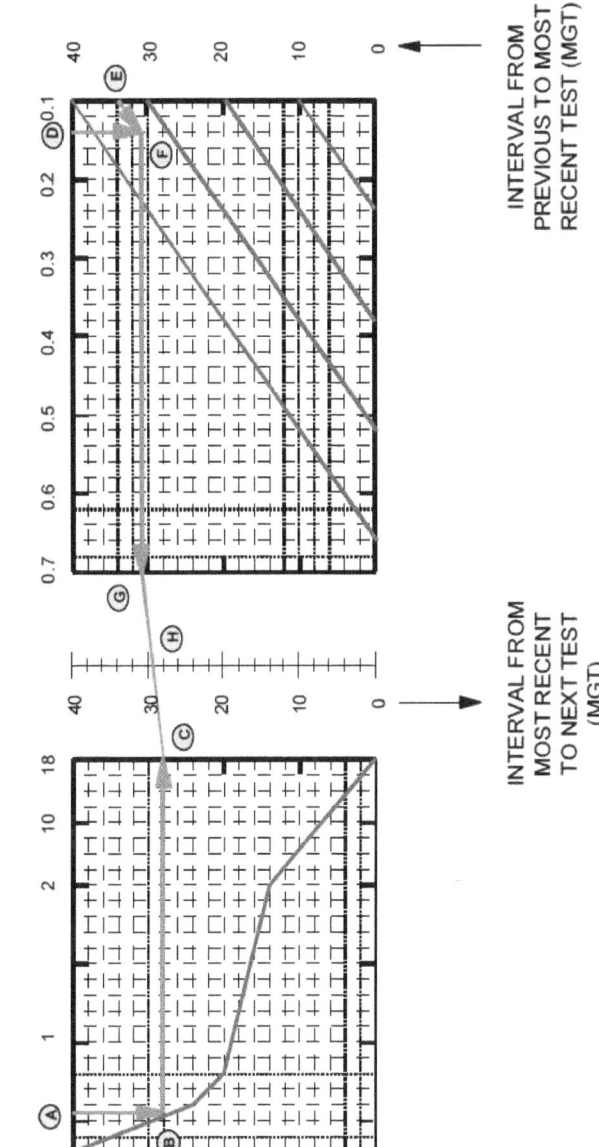

Figure 5. Hypothetical case to illustrate application of nomograph.

11

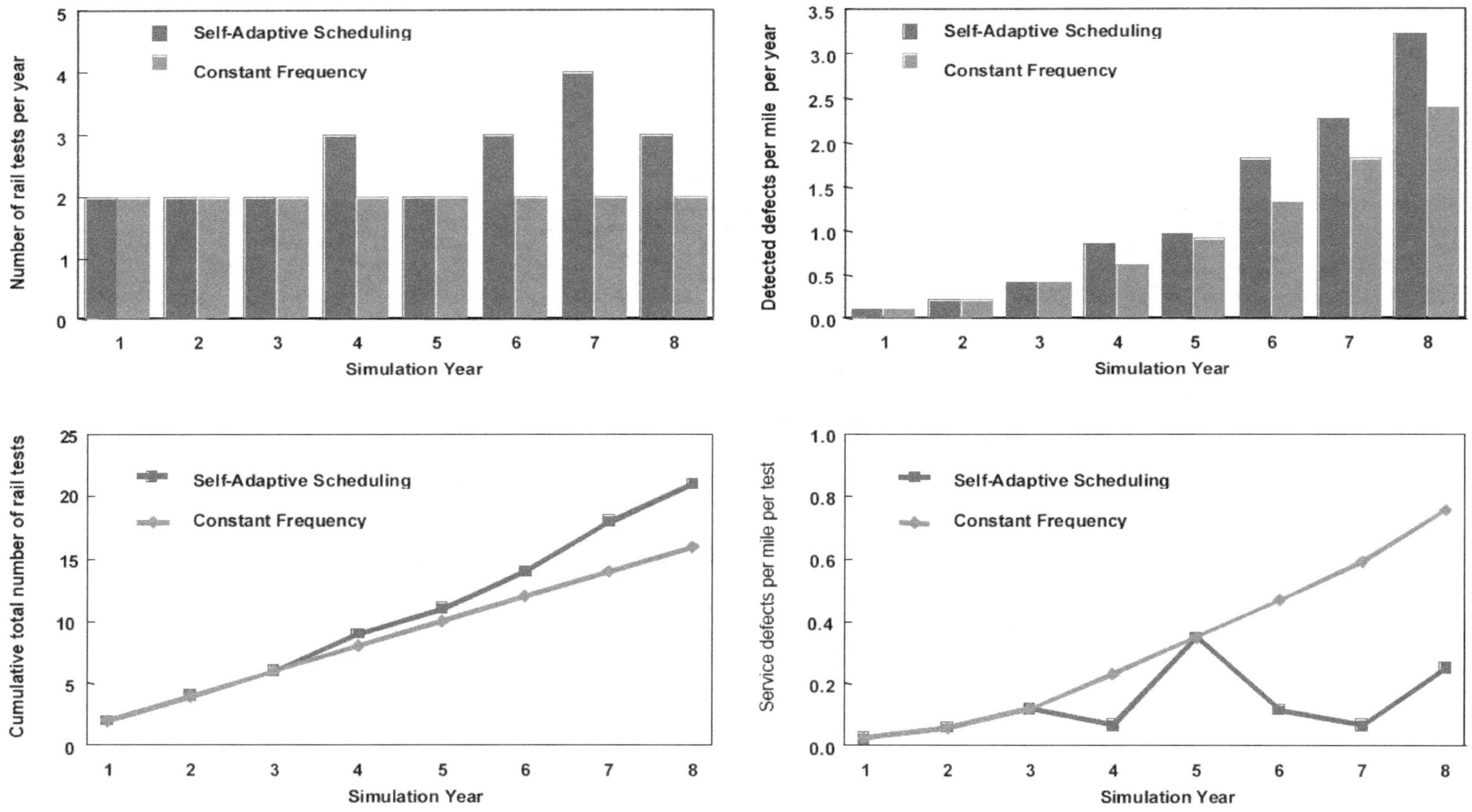

Figure 6. Simulation of rail testing on a hypothetical medium density line (60 MGT per year).

12

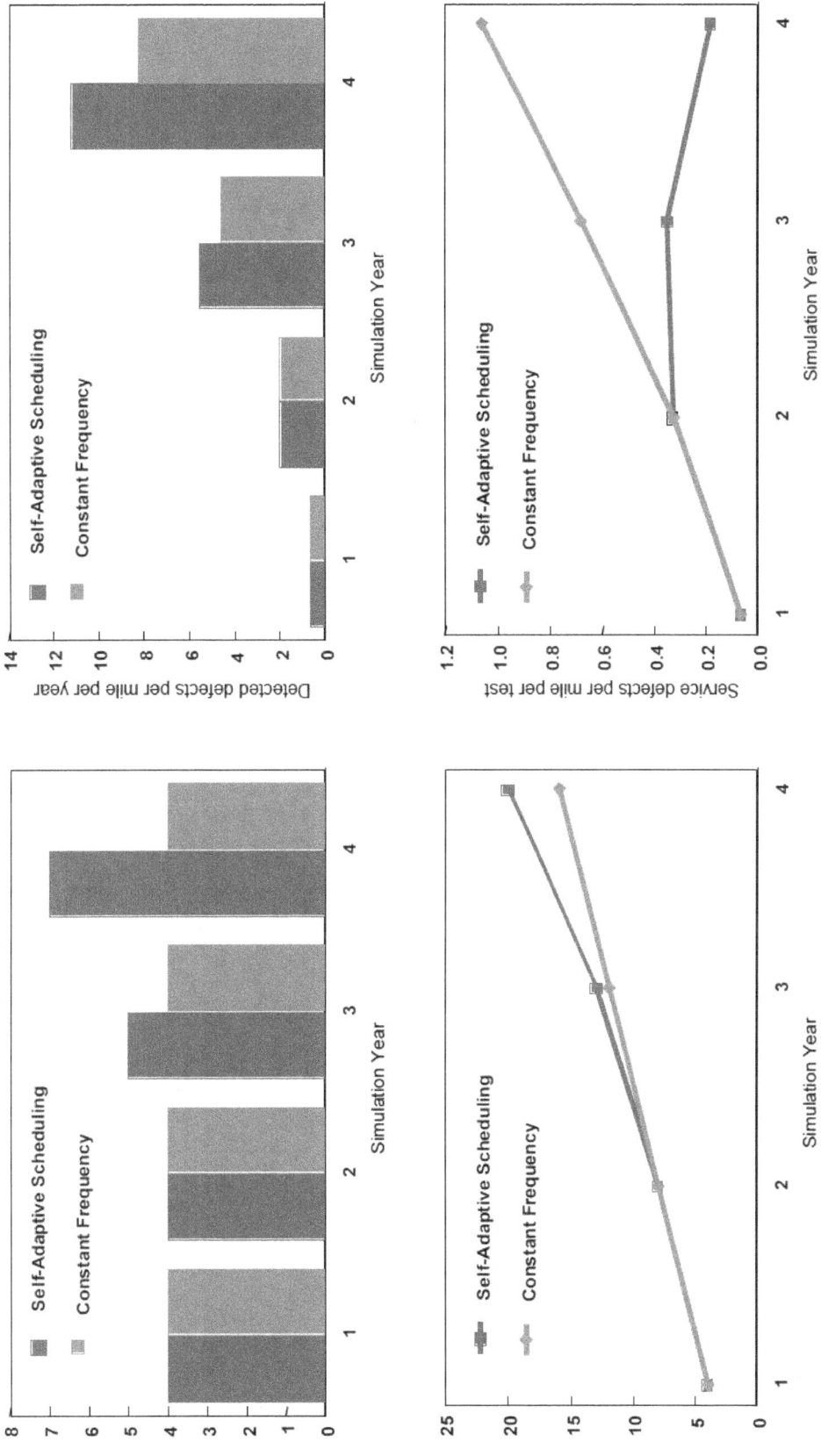

Figure 7. Simulation of rail testing on a hypothetical heavy haul line (120 MGT per year).

13

3.2 LIMITS ON RAIL HEAD WEAR

Wear is not a rail defect in the same sense as a crack, which is a stress raiser and intensifies the local state of stress, but it is a cause of rail removal. Wear reduces the overall cross-sectional area of the rail, which increases the magnitude of bending and normal stresses in the rail, thereby weakening the capacity of the rail to carry load. Moreover, lateral wear and abnormal vertical wear are included in the UIC Catalogue of Rail Defects.

A methodology to estimate limits for rail head wear has been developed based on engineering fracture mechanics principles (Jeong, et al., 1998). The methodology assumes that a worn rail contains a defect and that a rail inspection program is in place to detect such defects. The limits for rail head wear are based on the rate of defect growth, how often the rail is inspected, and the fracture toughness of the rail steel. The original methodology was used to estimate limits for vertical head-height loss, Δh, and for gage-face side wear, Δw, separately but it can be also applied to calculate limits for combined vertical and lateral rail head wear.

The methodology to estimate limits for rail head wear combines the results from two separate sets of calculations. The first set of calculations estimates limits for rail wear based on fracture toughness assuming a known defect size and a specific loading condition (i.e. dynamic wheel load and temperature difference from neutral are assumed). Figure 8 shows a schematic of this first set of calculations.

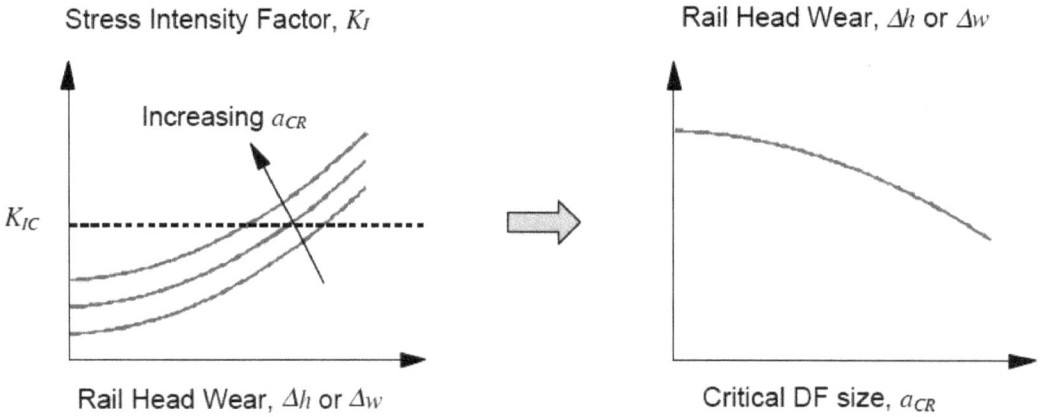

Figure 8. Schematic for estimating rail wear as a function of critical defect size.

Since the defect size is generally not known, a second set of calculations is performed to estimate the critical defect size that should be assumed to calculate limits on rail wear. The methodology assumes that rail wear reaches a limit when the defect grows from barely detectable size (assumed to be 5 %HA) to a critical size in less than one inspection interval (assumed to be 20 MGT). Figure 9 shows a schematic of the results from the second set of calculations which are based on the rail defect growth rate analyses.

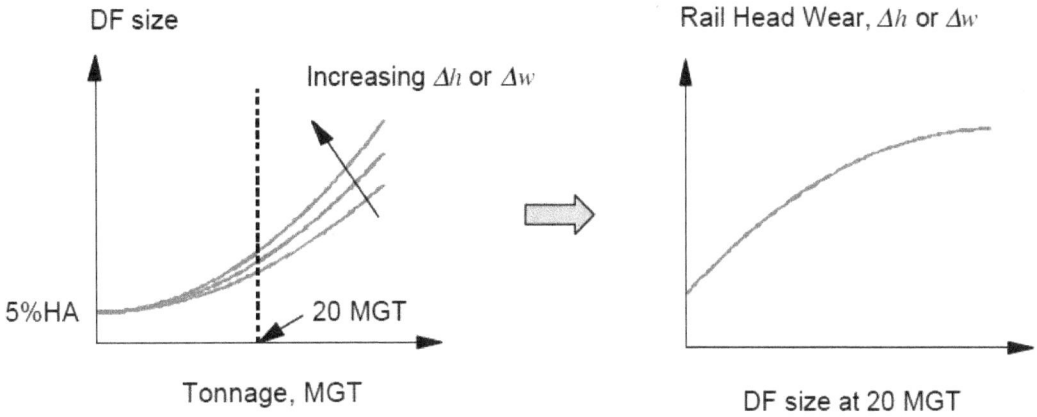

Figure 9. Schematic for estimating rail wear as a function of inspection interval.

The results of the two sets of calculations are combined to estimate limits for rail head wear (Figure 10). In other words, the intersection of the two curves; one based on fracture toughness and the other based on the defect growth rate; defines the limits for rail head wear.

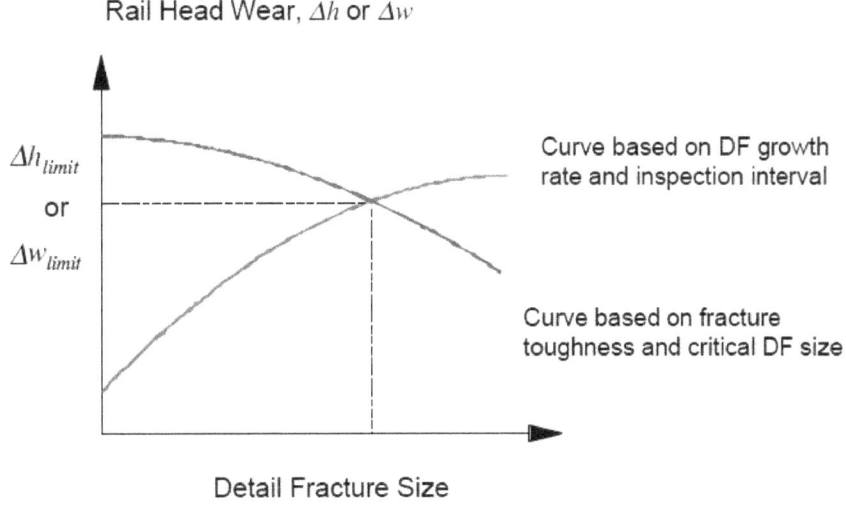

Figure 10. Estimate of rail wear limits based on fracture mechanics analysis.

Figure 11 compares wear limits used by a major railroad in the United States with those estimated by the fracture mechanics methodology for four different rail sections operating on FRA Class 5 track (maximum freight train speed of 80 miles per hour or approximately 133 kilometers per hour). In this figure, rail head wear is vertical head-

15

height loss. Similarly, Figure 12 shows a comparison for gage-face side wear. Both figures indicate that the wear limits estimated from the fracture mechanics methodology are less restrictive than those used in actual practice by this particular railroad. However, the limits shown for railroad practice may be based on economic considerations rather than, or in addition to, fracture strength. In establishing condemning limits for rail wear, other issues need to be taken into consideration in addition to fracture strength. For example,

- The vertical wear limit may be affected by wheel flange design, design of joint bars (including insulated joints), wheel-operated rail lubricators, etc.

- Side wear limit is affected by flange climb, vehicle dynamics (e.g., conicity and hunting), gauge widening, etc.

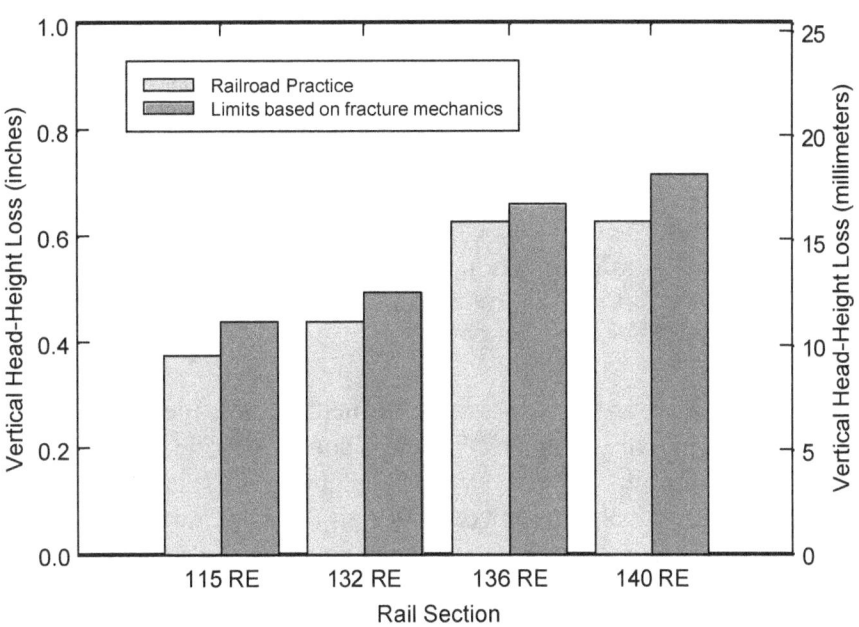

Figure 11. Actual and estimated limits for vertical head-height loss.

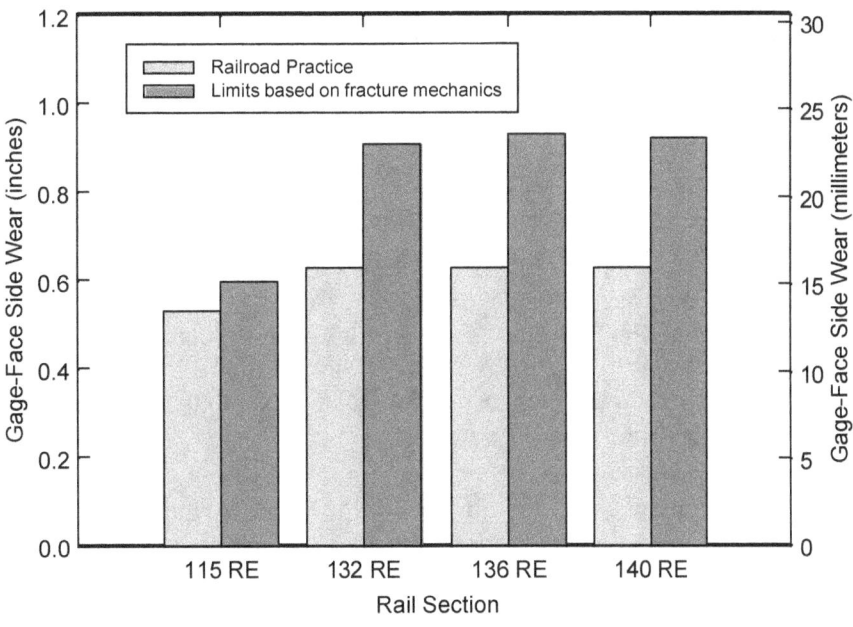

Figure 12. Actual and estimated limits for gage-face side wear.

3.3 RISK ANALYSIS

Risk analysis can be used as a decision-making tool to develop systematic improvements in track maintenance, inspection, and research strategies. Absolute safety of the track system cannot always be guaranteed due to uncertainties in system parameters, but the likelihood of unacceptable performance can be limited to a reasonable level with effective management strategies. This likelihood can be estimated using risk analysis.

Two examples of risk analyses are presented in this section to show how crack-growth life affects the frequency of rail inspection. The examples described here consider risk as the occurrence of service defects or broken rails. A cost/benefit analysis has not been included in these examples.

The first example of risk analysis is an assessment of an alternative rail inspection strategy to the present practice mandated by the Code of Federal Regulations (CFRs) in the United States. Current track safety standards require railroads to periodically inspect rail on lines where operating speeds exceed 40 mph (49 CFR Part 213.237) and to take immediate action to preserve operational safety whenever a rail defect is discovered (49 CFR Part 213.113). The immediate action may be a speed restriction, temporary repair, or permanent repair. Railroads generally make immediate repairs on heavy haul lines, in order to minimize disruption of revenue traffic, by organizing a chase gang to follow the inspection vehicle or detector car. Since the number of repairs per day is limited by chase-gang work rules and access to track between trains, the practice of immediate repair has led to restriction of detector car operations through territories with high concentrations of rail defects.

In reviewing its inspection records over a period of three years, a major railroad in the United States noted a decreasing trend in average daily track miles inspected. The railroad also noted a corresponding trend toward greater percentages of rail defects being discovered by means other than scheduled detector car operations. To reverse these trends without disrupting revenue traffic, the railroad proposed an alternative rail inspection strategy to the Federal Railroad Administration. For defects not exceeding a specified size, deferral of repair or other action would be permitted, provided that a follow-up gang completed the delayed action within a specified grace period. This would enable the detector car and chase gang to continue the inspection, thereby increasing the opportunity to find and repair larger defects. The proposal is consistent with earlier research results developed by the Volpe Center; namely, that rail defects tend to grow slowly and steadily under the influence of train loads, and that larger rail defects pose greater risks of rail failure than smaller defects.

A risk assessment model was developed by the Volpe Center (Tang, et al., 1995; Orringer et al., 1999) to evaluate this delayed action concept. In this evaluation, risk was defined as the occurrence of service defects; and benefit was defined as more efficient detector car utilization. The risk analysis is based on a Monte Carlo simulation of certain aspects of rail inspection on a hypothetical railroad subdivision of 1,000 miles.

Figure 13 shows results from the risk evaluation of two different rail inspection procedures. The abscissa is the detected defect rate (defects per mile per year) which defines a field condition. Also, PP represents the present practice for rail inspection, and DA represents delayed action. The figure shows that on a hypothetical railroad line carrying 60 MGT per year, the risk associated with 3 inspections per year is less than that for two inspections per year. The figure also shows that the delayed action procedure is no worse than the present practice in terms of service defects.

Figure 14 shows that higher inspection frequency leads to about 50% more car miles per day if present practice is followed. Since there is also a 50% increase in the number of inspections, this result implies no net change in the total number of car days required to complete the annual inspection program. Conversely, the higher inspection frequency leads to less than 50% extra car miles per day if delayed action is followed which leads to a modest increase in the number of days to complete an annual inspection program.

A second example of risk analysis shows the risks associated with changing the rail size on a hypothetical railroad line from 132 RE to 115 RE, or vise versa. Here again, risk is defined in terms of the service defect rate or the number of service defects per mile per year which are assumed to cause to rail failures. The risk analysis is based on the simulation model (Orringer, et al., 1999) used in the first example for risk analysis.

Figure 15 shows the crack-growth lives assumed in the risk analysis for 115 RE and 132 RE rails. The initial detail fracture size in these curves is 0.5 %HA; the size at which rail failure is expected to occur is 80%HA. The growth curves were derived from the engineering analysis model (Orringer et al., 1990) that was validated through the tests conducted during the UIC/WEC joint research project. Moreover, the figure indicates that slow crack-growth life of detail fractures in 115 RE rail is about 29% less than that in 132 RE.

In addition, the risk analysis assumes that the rate of crack formation is independent of rail size, and that only the growth rate is affected by changing rail size.[6]

Figure 16 shows the results from the Monte Carlo simulations for this hypothetical example in which the traffic density was 60 million gross tons per year. The frequency of inspection was varied in the simulations. Specifically, two different inspection intervals (twice a year and three times per year) were assumed for each of the two different rail sizes. Therefore, Figure 16 shows results from 4 different cases. In each case, the service defect rate increases somewhat linearly as the detected defect rate increases. If the number of inspections per year is not changed, changing the rail size from 132 RE to 115 RE will increase the service defect rate. Conversely, the risk of service defect occurrence can be mitigated by inspecting more frequently. For example, Figure 16 indicates that the service defect rate is slightly lower for 115 RE inspected three times a year than 132 RE rail inspected twice a year.

---

[6] Some defects, such as rolling contact fatigue cracks, are initiated and driven by the near surface wheel/rail contact stress field and residual stresses. Thus rail section does not necessarily affect their occurrence.

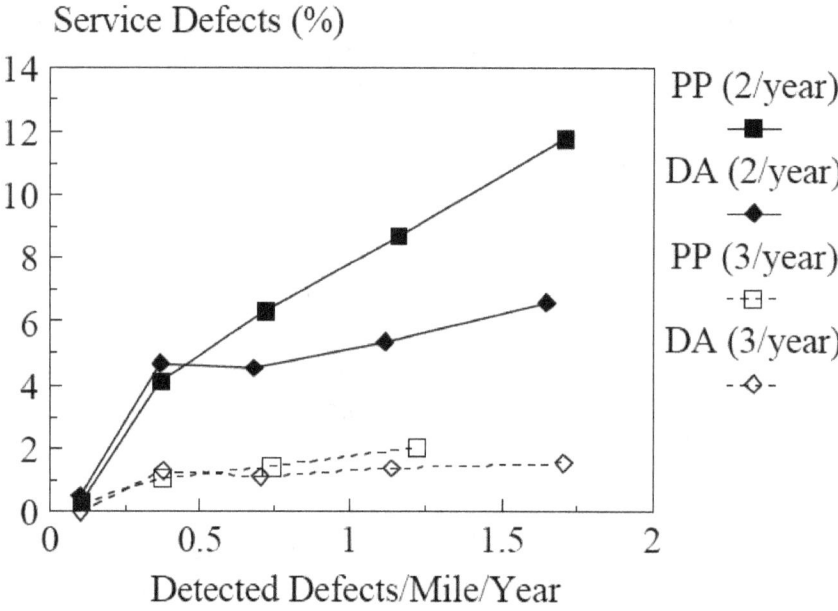

Figure 13. Effect of inspection interval on service defects for 60 MGT per year traffic density.

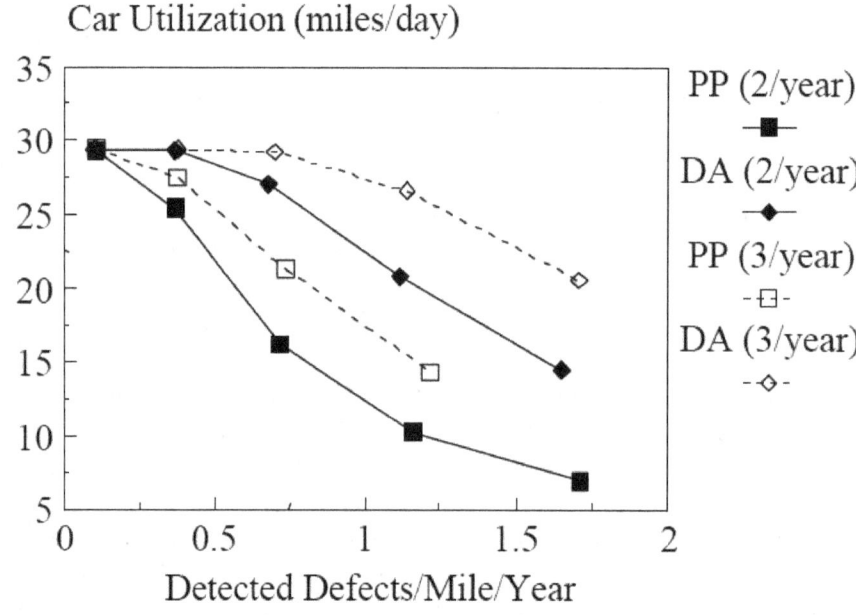

Figure 14. Effect of inspection interval on car utilization for 60 MGT per year traffic density.

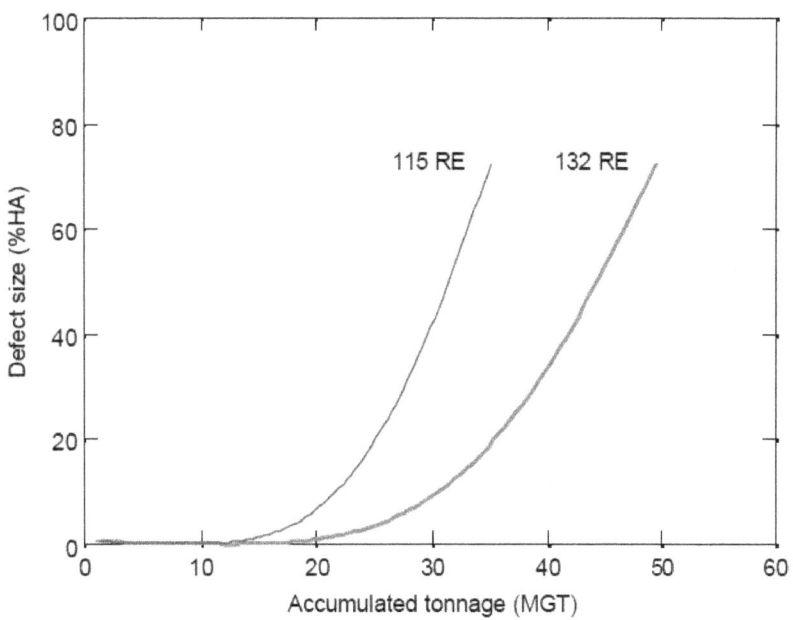

Figure 15. Comparison of assumed crack-growth curves for detail fractures in 115 RE and 132 RE rail.

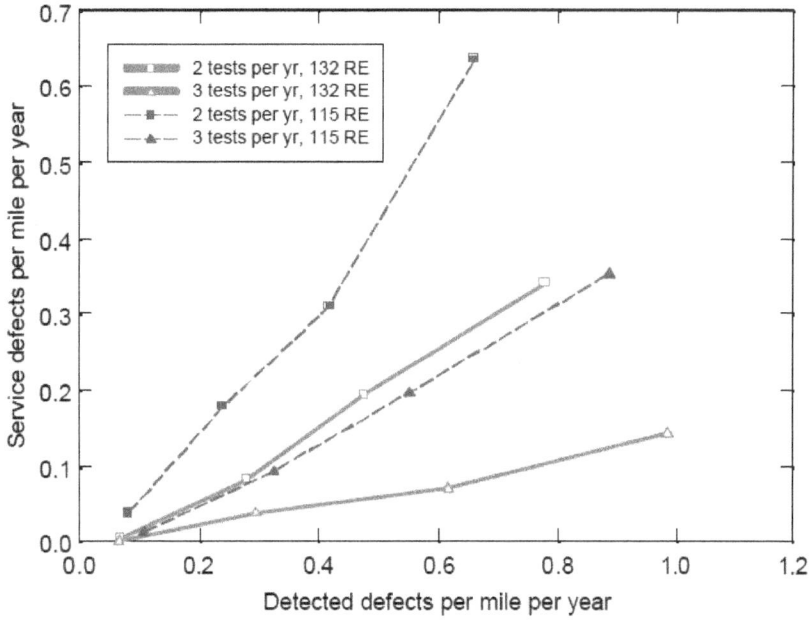

Figure 16. Effect of rail size and inspection frequency on service defect rate.

4. DISCUSSION

The UIC/WEC defect growth test program has focused on internal (e.g., detail fractures and tache ovale defects) and surface breaking defects (e.g., squat defects). Analysis of rail defects is based on engineering fracture mechanics principles which require fatigue crack-growth properties determined from laboratory tests using specially prepared test specimens. The analyses described in this three-part series of reports is based on fatigue crack-growth data from test specimens made from plain carbon rail steel (Scutti et al., 1984). As shown in the first report of this series (Jeong, 2002a), the Scutti et al. data are within the upper and lower bounds of fatigue crack-growth rates determined by the Office for Research and Experiments (ORE) of the International Union of Railways (ORE Question D156, 1985). Such tests should be performed using test specimens made from more modern rail (e.g., rail with head hardening). The process of head hardening, however, introduces complexities in the distribution of residual stress and in the microstructure within the rail head. Laboratory tests to determine the fatigue crack-growth properties in modern rail steel need to be designed to discriminate among the separate effects of stress intensity factor gradient, residual stress gradient, and microstructural gradient.

The engineering analyses to calculate detail fracture growth neglect the effects of load sequence. From a historical perspective, differences in the crack growth behavior of aircraft aluminum due to load sequence have been explained by crack closure.[7] However, results from analytical (Jeong and Sih, 1990; Sih and Jeong, 1992) and experimental studies (Jablonski and Pelloux, 1992) suggest that crack closure cannot entirely explain the differences in crack growth behavior of rail steels due to different load sequences. Thus, the cause of load sequence effects in rail steel remains an open question.

A validated analytical model can be used as a tool for failure analysis. For example, when a broken rail from an internal defect is found, the question is: what was the size of the defect at the last inspection? If the tonnage between the last rail test and the time of the rail break is known, the analytical model can be used to back-calculate the defect size at the last inspection.

Two examples of risk analysis were discussed previously in this report. Another example of risk analysis, which was not included here, could be to assess the effect of rail renewal on the risk of rail failures. The results of such a risk analysis could be used to estimate how often to renew rail and to develop effective strategies for rail renewal.

---

[7] Crack closure refers to a phenomenon that occurs when the opposing surfaces of a crack are in contact with each other. In the context of fatigue crack growth behavior, it is assumed that a crack does not propagate when the crack surfaces are in contact (i.e., during crack closure).

5. CONCLUSIONS

The contributions of the Federal Railroad Administration and the Volpe National Transportation Systems Center to the WEC/UIC joint research project have been described in a three-part series of reports. The first two reports described engineering analyses to correlate test data on the growth rates for various types of internal rail defects under laboratory and field conditions. This report discussed applications of the engineering model to rail defect management. The conclusions from the research described in these reports are summarized as follows.

Engineering fracture mechanics analyses were used to estimate the growth rate of rail head defects such as detail fractures, tache ovale defects, and squat defects. A stress intensity factor formula for squat defects was developed specifically for this project. The engineering analyses provide reasonable estimates of rail defect growth rates when correlated with test data obtained in the laboratory and in the field. The results from these correlations provide confidence in the engineering analysis model to estimate realistic growth rates for internal rail defects.

Guidelines for scheduling rail tests to detect internal rail defects can be developed using the results from test data and engineering analyses for defect growth. A guide for a such purpose was described in this report which was designed to adapt to a variety of changing conditions. Results from simulations show that the service defect rate between tests can be controlled by scheduling rail tests in accordance with actual track usage, defect experience, and detection equipment performance.

A rational methodology for estimating limits on rail head wear can be developed using fracture mechanics principles. However, in developing condemning limits for rail head wear other considerations need to be taken into account in addition to fracture strength (e.g., vehicle dynamics, lubrication, gauge widening, etc.)

The behavior of rail defect growth rates can be used in models for risk analysis. Results from risk analysis indicate that the delayed action concept has the potential to improve inspection efficiency without affecting the percentage of undetected defects. The results also suggest that the percentage of undetected defects can be reduced by increasing inspection frequency or by improving equipment performance. A cost/benefit analysis was not included in the analyses presented here.

REFERENCES

Besuner, P.M., D.H. Stone, M.A. DeHerrera, and K.W. Schoeneberg, 1978: "Statistical Analysis of Rail Defect Data (Rail Analysis – Volume 3)," AAR Chicago Technical Center, Report Number R-302.

Jablonski, D.A., and R.M. Pelloux, 1992: "Effect of train load spectra on crack growth in rail steel." *Residual Stresses in Rails, Vol. 1*, Kluwer Academic Publishers, The Netherlands, 81-98.

Jeong, D.Y., and G.C. Sih, 1990: "Evaluation of Elber's Crack Closure Model as an Explanation of Train Load Sequence Effects on Crack Growth Rates." Final Report: DOT/FRA/ORD-90/06.

Jeong, D.Y., 2002a: "Correlations Between Rail Defect Growth Test Data and Engineering Analyses, Part I: Laboratory Tests," Volpe Center Technical Report for the UIC/WEC Joint Research Project on Rail Defect Management.

Jeong, D.Y., 2002b: "Correlations Between Rail Defect Growth Test Data and Engineering Analyses, Part II: Field Tests," Volpe Center Technical Report for the UIC/WEC Joint Research Project on Rail Defect Management.

Jeong, D.Y., Y.H. Tang, and O. Orringer, 1998: "Estimation of Rail Wear Limits Based on Rail Strength Investigations," Volpe Center Final Report, DOT/FRA/ORD-98/07.

ORE Question D156, "Possibilities of improving the service characteristics of rails by metallurgical means," Report Number 2, Tests on used rails that failed in the track due to brittle fracture, Utrecht, September 1985.

Orringer, O., 1990: "Control of Rail Integrity By Self-Adaptive Scheduling of Rail Tests," Volpe Center Final Report, DOT/FRA/ORD-90/05.

Orringer, O., Y.H. Tang, J.E. Gordon, D.Y. Jeong, J.M. Morris, and A.B. Perlman, 1988: "Crack Propagation Life of Detail Fractures in Rails," Volpe Center Final Report, DOT/FRA/ORD-88/13.

Orringer, O., Y.H. Tang, D.Y. Jeong and A.B. Perlman, 1999: "Risk/Benefit Assessment of Delayed Remedial Action Concept for Rail Inspection," Volpe Center Final Report, DOT/FRA/ORD-99/03.

Scutti, J.J., R.M. Pelloux, and R. Fuquen-Moleno, 1984: "Fatigue behavior of a rail steel," *Fatigue & Fracture of Engineering Materials & Structures 7,* 121-135.

Sih, G.C., and D.Y. Jeong, 1992: "Effect of load sequence on fatigue life of rail steel." *Residual Stresses in Rails, Vol. 2,* Kluwer Academic Publishers, The Netherlands, 63-85.

Tang, Y.H., O. Orringer, and A.B. Perlman, 1995: "Simulation Model for Risk/Benefit Evaluation of Rail Inspection Programs," Volpe National Transportation Systems Center Report No. DOT-VNTSC-FRA-95-6.

Weibull, W., 1951, "A Statistical Distribution Function of Wide Applicability," *Journal of Applied Mechanics, Transactions of the American Society of Mechanical Engineers*, pp. 293-297.

www.ingramcontent.com/pod-product-compliance
Lightning Source LLC
Chambersburg PA
CBHW081808280526
45789CB00008B/3049